Literacy in Nursery Education

Literacy in Nursery Education

Robin Campbell

Trentham Books

First published in 1996 by Trentham Books Limited

Trentham Books Limited
Westview House
734 London Road
Oakhill
Stoke-on-Trent
Staffordshire
England ST4 5NP

British Cataloguing in Publication Data
A catalogue record for this book is available from the British Library
ISBN: 1 85856 064 0

Designed and typeset by Trentham Print Design Ltd., Chester
and printed in Great Britain by Bemrose Shafron Limited, Chester

Contents

Acknowledgements

The writing of this book was greatly helped by support from three sources. First, my work at the University of Hertfordshire ensured that I was in regular contact with early years classrooms. The teachers in those classrooms and the students learning in those environments, as well as my colleagues, were all indirectly informing me of literacy practices in nursery classrooms. More directly, the children in many nursery classrooms constantly demonstrated factors about their literacy learning and suggested important features of this book.

Finally, my wife Ruby, an early years teacher, was working in a nursery classroom while this book was being written. Her contribution to the development of this book was very influential as she informed, questioned and evaluated various parts of the text.

Chapter 1

Introduction

Until very recently literacy development would not have been among the top priorities for the nursery classroom. The nursery years would have been seen as a time when children were encouraged to explore the classroom to develop physically, intellectually, emotionally, socially and morally. Accordingly the provision of opportunities for play were, and still need to be, a key aspect of the nursery classroom provision. Reading and writing might, then, have been seen as more appropriately learned in the years beyond the nursery classroom. Such a view can no longer be accepted.

Part of the reluctance to encourage reading and writing in the nursery classroom may have been linked to notions of reading readiness. Downing and Thackray (1971) noted that the reading readiness concept suggested that certain abilities, skills and understandings were deemed necessary before children could begin to read. Unfortunately, for some children that meant that the provision of literacy materials or activities and of literacy support by teachers was being delayed until the children could demonstrate those particular attributes.

Two linked sources of information call into question such restrictions on children's opportunities to explore literacy in the nursery classroom. First, a growing number of books reported on children's reading and writing development before starting school (e.g. Bissex, 1980). Second, the concept of emergent literacy recognised the early and self-motivated learning of children about literacy (e.g. Hall, 1987). Both these sources indicated that literacy should have a higher profile. Indeed, these sources suggest that literacy learning for many children was well established before they entered the nursery classroom. Far from waiting for children to become ready to read, nursery teachers would need, instead, to be building on foundations already established at home.

The reports of children's reading and writing development before starting school have typically been written by the parents of these children – often academic staff of universities. If there were just one such book then the validity of the data or the exceptional nature of the child might be put forward to question the findings. However, with such a wealth of texts to consider, the strength of the argument that young children were learning about literacy and were reading and writing in some recognisable form, was confirmed.

For instance Bissex's book *Gnys at Wrk (Bissex,* 1980) highlighted in a dramatic way the early writing produced by Paul. The title itself emphasised the way in which young children develop their own knowledge of letters and sounds as a means of producing their first writing. Such learning was confirmed in the study of Adam (Schickedanz, 1990). In particular, as we might expect, children are prepared to spend a considerable amount of time experimenting with and exploring the letter shapes and sounds which make their own name (most usually forename). So, if we observe very young children we can note in their scribbles the appearance of letters from their forenames. Subsequently those letters will be grouped in a way which resembles the conventional form and eventually the child will write his/her name accurately.

Baghban (1984) provided a literacy study of her daughter, Giti, from birth to three. Her study also showed the development of writing from earlier 'scribbles' to subsequent use of letter-like shapes produced in a line. Furthermore, the study demonstrated Giti's involvement in shared readings of books including the naming of objects, at least early in her second year, as Giti took part in the conversations centred on a book. The study by Spreadbury (1994) also emphasized that parents will engage in lengthy conversations with their children focused on a book. For instance, when Scott Spreadbury shared a book with his mother at fourteen months she asked him twenty-one questions even though he couldn't yet respond with words. The questions appeared to be designed to involve him in the reading and get him to point to objects in the illustrations, rather than requiring answers. The numerous additional comments by his mother also appeared to involve him in the reading of the book.

So the early literacy development of these children (and many others like them) came from opportunities to write at home and from the story readings and shared readings of books with a parent or other significant adult. However, it also developed from the children's awareness of environmental print and from their parents' willingness to talk about that print (Laminack, 1991). Many examples are given of Zachary Laminack talking with his parents about the print in his environment. Not unexpectedly, Zachary wanted to make sense of the world in which he lived. In our modern western culture, this frequently includes trying to make sense of the print and its associated background in the environment.

Derived from these and earlier studies of young children developing as literacy learners, and from other studies of young children engaging with literacy (e.g. Goodman, 1990), the notion of emergent literacy became recognised. Studies of emergent literacy (e.g. Hall, 1987 and Strickland and Morrow, 1989) tell us that young children are learning to read and write very early in life. Although it is difficult to identify how soon this process can begin, by one year of age many children demonstrate that it is well in place. Such learning will not follow a clearly defined sequence but will be derived from learning in real life settings where the literacy serves a purpose, or need, for the child. And that learning will involve the active engagement of the children trying to make sense of their world. Most frequently, the children will be supported in that learning by an adult who helps them in various ways with the print that interests them.

During the first year of life it might be the ability to manipulate and use a book (especially the less fragile hardboard books) that is the most obvious sign of emergent literacy. Holding and using a pencil, or similar object for creating a mark, is a more difficult operation. Beyond the first year and before beginning school, reading and writing will be developing side by side, each supporting the other. So, if all that is happening, what does it suggest for the nursery classroom?

The adults working in the nursery classroom will want to build upon literacy learning by providing a good many meaningful activities that involve reading and writing. Such activities will also meet the needs of children who have had less opportunity to engage with literacy. The teacher will not be excluding the important play activities but simply adding opportunities and activities to support the children in their literacy development.

The teacher's objective will be to get children actively involved in reading and writing, focusing on the child's learning about literacy. The classroom can be arranged, managed and developed in ways that ensure that the children can explore literacy. While not directly and didactically teaching reading and writing there will be a need for teachers to engage in providing, reading, modelling, interacting and talking about literacy.

This book sets out to explore what the teacher and other adults might do to ensure that the nursery classroom is rich in literacy activities and opportunities that encourage and support children learning about reading and writing, and (at least in part) to help them learn to read and write.

Chapter two considers the roles of the teacher and other adults in providing opportunities for literacy. This might appear to be easy since it merely requires making adjustments to the classroom provision so as to facilitate the literacy possibilities for the children – but in reality it is never simple because it requires the adults to make judgements about how the provision might best meet the needs of the children. Chapter three looks at a frequent feature of early childhood education, both at home and at school, namely reading stories. The importance of this activity is well documented and we shall look at its benefits for literacy. Chapter four describes the modelling of literacy during story reading and in shared book experience: shared reading and writing is also described. Chapter five takes account of the fact that the provision, reading and modelling of literacy leads to various kinds of interaction and explores a number of activities where teacher and children interact with literacy. Using nursery rhymes and songs as part of the nursery classroom tradition is discussed in chapter six, and chapter seven looks at how teachers can maintain an interest in literacy in the classroom by talking about environmental and classroom print. The concluding chapter draws some of these strands together in the context of nursery classroom principles.

Chapter 2

Providing opportunities for literacy

The first task for the adults in the nursery classroom is to ensure that there really are literacy opportunities for the children. The play area or home corner can be a starting point where the scope for literacy can be widened. Next, a writing centre or writing table can be established. Many nursery classrooms have a painting table or painting area where children can use a variety of materials to create a picture and they could be given similar opportunities to write. Finally, this chapter considers the library corner, a regular feature of the early years classroom. Here we explore its potential as part of the nursery classroom environment designed to attract children to books.

Play area

The play area is a well established part of the nursery classroom provision, because of the wealth of learning that can be created from play. It creates opportunities for make-believe and use of the imagination, it requires children to reason, make judgements and engage in thinking about the situations in which they are taking part. As well as encouraging cognitive development, the play area is also likely to support physical development as children manipulate the various small and large objects provided. Since it is unusual for the children to play in isolation there are opportunities for cognitive and physical growth and, moreover, the social development of the children will be enhanced as they relate to, and co-operate with, other children.

If the materials and the setting for the play remain unchanged over long periods of time, play can become stilted. So the teacher has an important role in providing new materials which can suggest other settings for the play and also discussing with the children the possibilities offered by the new equipment (Manning and Sharp, 1977).

Further, the possibilities for play activities can be extended by adding appropriate literacy materials which encourage children to read or pretend read and to write, even though initially some of the writing might look like scribbles. Books, magazines and brochures can be added to the play area for the teacher to select according to the way in which the play area is being used: a wide range of magazines in the waiting area of the 'dentist's' or a more restricted emphasis on car, caravan and motor-bike magazines in the 'garage'. There could be magazines, telephone directories, notices, instructions and forms and also notepads, paper and envelopes and a variety of pencils, crayons, coloured pencils and felt-tip pens for writing.

Of course, the teacher does not just provide the materials and then leave the children to discover the possibilities on their own but needs to visit the play area and model literacy behaviours by using the available materials, for example, putting a telephone message pad and a pencil next to the telephone and then making a few notes when talking on the phone. In one nursery classroom where this was done the three and four year old children soon became regular writers of notes after using the telephone. At first the message pad contained scribbles, which could not be identified as attempts at writing or drawing. However, there were also, among the scribbles, single letters or shapes which approximated to letters. Other pages had lines of letters which, although clearly designed to be writing, were not easily decipherable into a message. So, over a period of time the children produced more writing with letters, and lines of letters, and eventually their efforts became less scribble and more like writing.

However, much more is needed than just a telephone message pad. The entire play area can be adapted to widen the opportunities for play and create a variety of possibilities for literacy. Morrow and Rand (1991) describe in some detail the organisation of the play area as veterinarians' offices and indicate how this can provide literacy possibilities such as appointment cards, patient forms, prescription pads, telephone messages and pet books. They go on to list other possible settings that can be arranged to vary the play and widen the scope for literacy. Hall and Abbott (1991) similarly illustrate a range of settings for play and literacy in which children developed as literacy users. They include examples provided by class teachers who describe how they worked together with children on literacy through play.

Potential settings are numerous. Some are very general and can be linked to children's experiences – a supermarket or grocery shop, a dentist's office, a petrol station. Others, such as a travel agency or airport, might be less familiar. Knowing the children and the local environment will enable teachers to determine what might be suitable, perhaps in discussion with the children. Each setting should give scope for the children to play and to link literacy to that play.

Writing centre

As already suggested, many nursery classrooms might have a painting table or painting area where children can use a variety of materials to create a picture. This allows them to represent what they have observed or imagined. Initially some representations will look more like scribbles than a conventional, or even unconventional representation of an object. Such scribbles are part of the process of learning to represent. As children begin to appreciate the nature of print so, too, they attempt to create writing. The children can be encouraged in their endeavours by being offered several different settings and opportunities for writing. We have seen that the play area can be a setting and an opportunity for writing. A writing centre can do the same.

With the development and acceptance of process writing in the 1980s (see for instance Graves, 1983), the advantages of a writing centre as part of a primary school classroom organisation became widely recognised. Morrow (1989) suggests that in pre-school and early years classrooms too, writing centres would support literacy development. Assuming that some form of integrated day would be in operation a writing centre provides the setting for children to write on a regular and frequent basis. The examples provided from a reception classroom (SCDC, 1989) and a nursery classroom (Campbell, 1995b) suggest that a writing centre can be used productively with young children.

A writing centre requires simply a table and some chairs – no more than six – and a selection of paper of different sizes, colours and shapes that varies daily, with new materials added regularly: pencils, crayons, chalks and felt pens and sometimes charcoal. The children need to be aware that they can visit the writing centre to write whenever there is a vacant chair.

The teacher or other adults in the classroom need to visit the writing centre to support the children with their writing. They might suggest what the children could write about, related perhaps to objects, events, or visits to or from the classroom, although often the children will prefer to write about something of immediate importance to themselves. Teachers, too, can write at the writing centre. By writing alongside the children teachers are able to provide a demonstration of writing which could help the children. They can also act as an audience for the writing produced by the children. Whenever possible, teachers try to read the child's writing unaided but often ask the children to read their own writing to make sure that the message is not misrepresented. All this encourages children to think about writing and to think of themselves as writers.

The range of writing produced at the writing centre by three and four year old nursery children demonstrates a wide range of understanding about writing. In the nursery classroom where the children were observed at the writing centre (Campbell, 1995b) there were examples of:

Scribbles: in particular, circles and ovals usually produced with large sweeps of the pencil, which might have been attempts to write. However, they were not easily distinguishable from other scribbles which children described as drawings.

David's scribble was, he told his teacher, 'Santa Claus'.

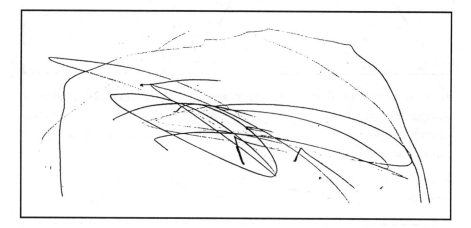

Linear scribbles: although not containing any letters or letter-like shapes, this writing began to display some linearity. Such lines of scribbles were most usually on a horizontal plane.

Laureen produced a linear scribble 'About my house'.

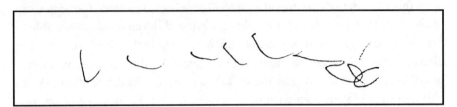

Psuedo-letters: the linear scribbles will often include letter-like shapes. That is, they display the vertical and horizontal lines, circles, semi-circles and arcs which are found in letters but also other squiggles and they are not recognisable as alphabetic letters.

Kimberly produced a page of psuedo-letters which she told her teacher was 'About my holiday'.

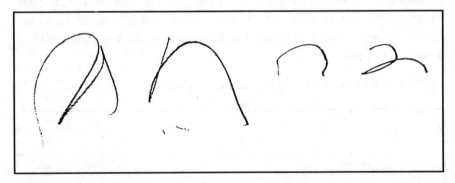

Actual letters: in the lines of psuedo-letters, alphabetic letters will gradually emerge. Eventually all or most of the writing will contain actual letters, although they may not connect easily with the spoken message used by the child to describe it.

Aashish wrote a line of letters which he said was 'My mum being busy at work' but which actually emphasised letters from his own forename.

Own name: among the letters used in children's writing there are often letters from their forename, or their complete forename will appear at intervals throughout the writing.

Amy did not tell her teacher about her writing but we can see repetitions of her forename.

Invented spellings: children take an important step forward when they obviously attempt to use sounds and associated letters to construct the writing. The first letter of words most usually appear in the writing. It is at this point that teachers, with skill and care, are able to read the writing produced.

Laureen's writing was 'Mum, Charlie and Dad' and was produced just over two months after her linear scribble. The first letter was evident in each of her words and other letters created a reasonable or accurate representation of each word that she wrote.

Conventional words: as some words become established in the child's visual memory they appear in the writing in a conventional and accurate format. For some children these words will be surrounded by other invented spellings, but a few children will begin to restrict themselves to words which they know to be accurate.

Ricky wrote 'My name and car' but declined to write anything further.

Although such descriptions of children's writing (e.g. Temple et al, 1988) can be useful as a guide to what they might produce and how they might next develop in their writing, children in reality move back and forth between such stages as they explore print. The growth towards literacy is not straightforward. Nevertheless, such features of children's early writing do provide a framework for us to observe children as writers and affirms the benefits of the writing centre which provides the opportunity for the child to write regularly and frequently.

Library corner

A customary feature of early years classrooms is a library corner, as a survey of 470 primary classrooms in the UK shows (HMI, 1991). Most nursery classrooms also have a library corner. It can serve a number of purposes, from the simple storage of books to a means of attracting children to books, a quiet area for the children to engage with books, a resource to support links with home, and a setting for story readings.

At the simplest level the library corner provides an area for the storage of books. It needs to be attractively organised and carefully positioned in the classroom. Most usually, a corner of the room provides two walls of the library and partitions and shelves the remainder. The shelves and bookcases used to store the books should carry a tempting display. Books should be displayed face forward, so that the covers attract the children.

Other attractions of the library corner can include posters depicting a story or characters from a story, and stuffed toy versions of well-loved story characters, (Campbell, 1992). Following class story readings, some children might, individually or in a group, make pictures about the story, which can in turn also be displayed in the library corner. The library corner should look appealing because of the books and the relevant surroundings and displays. A soft carpet on the floor, comfortable chairs, large bean bags and perhaps a sofa all add to the appeal of the library corner.

A quiet, comfortable and attractive library corner of this kind is designed to produce the setting for children to engage with books. Denny Taylor (1983), in her studies of young children learning to read at home, noted that pre-school children frequently have momentary engagements with print. The child may sit and look through a book before moving off once again to explore the physical environment of the home. Such engagements are encouraged and supported where there is a collection of print, or books, and a quiet and comfortable setting. Naturally, it requires the teacher to model and support the engagement with a book by reading stories and providing shared readings and shared book experiences and by visiting the library corner to demonstrate involvement with a particular book.

The books in the library corner also provide a resource for making constructive links with home. Children can select a book from the library corner, leave the book card in a wall-hanging pocket with their forename on it, and take the book home to share it. Some parents may require guidance on the nature of such shared readings, so that they emphasise the enjoyment of the shared reading and the talk about the pictures. It can be suggested that the adult reads the book aloud, invites comments from the child and perhaps encourages the child to retell the story or draw a picture about it. When the book is returned a brief discussion between child and teacher or nursery nurse about the book and what the child felt about it, can complete this link with home.

Finally, although the library corner will be designed to accommodate small groups of children, teachers in nursery classrooms might prefer that one boundary is open, to allow the whole class to come together there occasionally. This comfortable environment be used to plan or review the events of the day as well as being the hub of literacy development, where the children expect to have their shared book experience or enjoy nursery rhymes and songs. The library corner might well be used on a daily basis for the teacher to read or tell a story to the children. Story readings are of such importance to the children that they deserve a chapter to themselves.

Chapter 3

Reading stories

All the evidence suggests that reading stories to young children regularly and frequently is very important. Young children at home benefit in many ways from having stories read to them. Bernice Cullinan in her forword to Taylor and Strickland (1986) asserts unequivocally that: 'Those (children) who have stories read to them will become readers...' (p.x). Teachers and other adults in the nursery classroom who read stories to children are continuing the beneficial home literacy practice which many children experience.

The evidence supporting the value of reading stories to children is derived from a number of sources. First, there are studies of individual children that document the importance given by particular parents to reading stories to their own children. A number were mentioned in the introduction to this book (e.g. Baghban, 1984). An earlier more detailed account, specifically about story reading, is by Dorothy White (1954), a children's librarian. She describes it as a reading diary. It gives a vivid account of the books that she read to her daughter Carol, and indicates the child's response to and involvement with those stories. The diary entries build up a clear picture of the development of a reader as stories are read regularly and frequently – and repeatedly – to the child.

Second, there are the books which provide information on groups of children who have developed along the road to reading, or are reading, before they start school. Taylor and Strickland (1986) concentrate upon story reading in family contexts indicating how this practice enables children to develop as readers. Unlike many of the books written about young children developing as readers, Taylor and Strickland provide accounts of children from a wide variety of family backgrounds who have story books read to them by their parents. It is clearly not only the children of teachers and librarians who have benefited from story readings. Likewise, Clark (1976) demonstrates that children from a wide variety of family backgrounds can become fluent readers before starting school. A number of factors might have contributed to the thirty-two children in her study becoming fluent readers so early. She highlights the importance of an interested adult answering the child's questions and the use of story readings to encourage the children towards reading.

Third, there are studies which report on large numbers of children and attempt to isolate key factors leading to success, such as the longitudinal Children Learning to Read project in Bristol, led by Gordon Wells. He concluded that listening to stories read aloud and being able to take part in discussions about them was an important contribution to children's subsequent literacy development (Wells, 1986).

All these studies note the positive effects of the use of story readings with young children. Bill Teale's (1984) survey of these and other studies led him to conclude that story reading facilitated literacy development. So there is good reason why adults in the nursery classroom should read stories to children on a daily basis. Some of the specific benefits that appear to accrue from such story readings merit detailed consideration.

At the simplest level, perhaps, are the physical attributes that are learnt from story readings. As Strickland and Morrow (1989) note, children learn how to handle books. Both front-to-back and left-to-right directionality need to be observed so that children can become aware of and understand these features of English print in books. Children who are becoming literate in Urdu or Arabic, for example, will be accustomed to print that is read from right to left. But, of course, story readings do much more than this: they teach about language. As Henrietta Dombey (1988) has argued, children learn new words, new syntactic forms, new meanings and new ways of organising discourse from nursery classroom story readings. Not only do children extend their vocabulary through stories, then, but their understanding of how to organise this vocabulary is enhanced. Enhancement of their language is important because it enables children to read the same book for themselves later and to read other books.

In addition to enhancing language, story reading supports emotional, social and psychological development (Trelease, 1984) because stories provide an opportunity for children to think about experiences and events beyond their own experiences. In particular, the motives, behaviours and feelings of the characters in a story help children to understand their own more comprehensively. Furthermore, Shelby Anne Wolf indicated in her study of her two daughters, Lindsey and Ashley (Wolf and Heath, 1992), that they frequently used stories, and the characters from stories as part of their imaginative play. What will be evident in the play area of the nursery classroom is how characters and events from stories are used by children to support their thinking and play.

Story readings need to be a part of the daily life of the nursery classroom not for directly teaching children to read but for facilitating children's growth towards literacy. Importantly, too, reading stories to children can create interest in and enjoyment of reading and this encourages children ultimately to become readers themselves.

Where story readings are an important part of the nursery classroom day, teachers select books with care. Jim Trelease (1984) suggests that teachers should only read stories they themselves enjoy, because the enjoyment of the story has to be evident in the reading. Many teachers develop a familiarity with favourite books so that story reading appears more like story telling, the teacher only glancing at the text as she shows the pictures, emphasises certain parts, maintains eye contact with the children and captures their interest.

Children too play their part in the reading. They comment on the story, ask questions and relate the story to their own experiences. The story reading becomes interactive – or as Dombey (1988) suggests, the children become 'partners in the telling' (p75): the children interject and the teacher uses these interjections and then moves the story forward. Crucially, she does not reject the children's comments because they are constructing their own meanings by taking part in the story reading.

Teachers usually prepare children before reading the book. They might, as Meek (1988) suggests, discuss the cover and some of the illustrations and learn about the characters. Or they might discuss the author, publisher and other features of the book. But the central feature of the reading is the story itself. Any discussion about the book is for the purpose of helping the children to be involved in the story reading.

In one nursery classroom the teacher talked briefly with her class of twenty six three and four year olds, about *The Very Hungry Caterpillar* (Carle, 1969) before she began to read it:

Teacher	Now, this book today is about a ...
Nikki	A snake.
Teacher	... caterpillar. He does look a bit like a snake.
	But it is a caterpillar.
Nikki	It does look like a snake.
Jamie	It's a caterpillar.
Teacher	And he was a very hungry caterpillar.
Steven	He needs to eat lots of food.
Ricky	He'll get fat.
Teacher	There's the caterpillar, can you see him?
Children	Yeah.
Teacher	But, before he was a caterpillar ...
John	He was tiny.
Teacher	He was small.
John	I can see him.

Teacher   Mmh.

In the light of the moon

a little egg lay on a leaf.

In this brief discussion the scene was set, at least in part, for the story. Another time the teacher might get the children to predict what happens in the story. Or the book to be read might already be a favourite and teacher and children could share memories of previous readings before the reading begins. But once into the story, the teacher should read it with care, emphasis and appropriate intonation, pausing so that the children remain with the story and create their own meanings.

During the reading of *The Very Hungry Caterpillar*, the children joined in at times and commented upon the story and the main character:

Teacher   *On Wednesday*

he ate through

three plums.

Josie   He'll get a belly-ache.

Jamie   He ate too many foods.

Teacher   *but he was still*

hungry.

Children   *but he was still*

hungry.   (Read as an echo of the teacher and just behind her).

Teacher   He will get a stomach-ache won't he?

One of the features of this story is the repetition of the sentence 'But he was still hungry'. Even very young children soon get to know the phrase and the part it plays in the rhythm of the story and are quick to join in with this. In a sense, the rhythm acts as an invitation to the children to join in the story reading – and turns them into readers as they utter the words. Josie and Jamie also comment upon what was happening and their comments indicate that they have heard the story before or were able to predict some of the outcomes based on their own experiences. The teacher acknowledged one of their comments, agreeing with the outcome they predict. She also puts her acknowledgement and acceptance of the child's comment into the language of the book, saying 'stomach-ache' rather than belly-ache.

After she finished the story, the teacher talked with the children about the food that caterpillars need and the reason why this caterpillar got a stomach-ache:

Teacher   So what food did the caterpillar need to eat?

Children   Leaf.

Alan   They eat the plants in the garden.

Teacher   They do. What part do they eat?

Alan   The leaves.

Teacher   That's right. And what did this caterpillar do in the story?

Nikki   He had the wrong foods.

Jamie   That was for boys.

Nikki   And girls.

Teacher   Yes, he was eating the foods that we have, wasn't he?

A quiz about all aspects of the story that has just been read is to be avoided. But a brief discussion which allows the children to comment upon the plot, the behaviour of the characters, and their own feelings about the story can help ensure that meanings have been taken in. As noted earlier, some children will then use the stories to enhance their play. Furthermore, echoes from stories read aloud may be heard subsequently in the children's use of language.

Many nursery teachers find that so much is developed from story readings that they choose to start the day with one. The story reading is used as the basis for bringing the children together and providing some ideas to inform their play, and the painting or the use of large equipment during the rest of the day. This may seem a rather formal start to the day (and some teachers will prefer story readings at different times in the day) but, as Henrietta Dombey (1988) observes it provides formality of context, inside which can lie an informality of process as the children interject their thoughts. During the process of story reading it 'is the rule of relevance' (p81) for the children which governs the interactive nature of the story readings. Embedded in these interactive story readings is the actual reading (or modelling) of the words in print. And the modelling of literacy is an important part of the role for nursery staff.

Chapter 4

Modelling literacy

Demonstrations of literacy, it has been argued, are an important part of classroom life (Cambourne, 1988) and they can certainly be developed in the nursery classroom. During demonstrations the teacher, or other adult, will frequently be modelling reading or writing for the children, to help them construct a concept of literacy activities. After all, how would children learn about the nature of reading and writing if they had never witnessed them taking place?

Many of the children starting nursery school have been read to at home and, perhaps, helped(!) a parent construct a shopping list, so have already witnessed reading and writing being modelled. New observations of reading and writing taking place in another context, and with other adults, will nevertheless add to their learning. Children not thus advantaged and for whom reading and writing are new need even more to see literacy being modelled. Whatever their past experience, each child will extract from the modelling the awareness or knowledge which he/she requires at that moment about reading and writing.

The adults in the nursery classroom model reading and writing at various times in the activities centred upon a book, whether it be story reading, shared book experience or shared reading.

Story reading

Story reading is such an important literacy activity that a chapter has explored the range of learning that appears to take place when children hear stories read to them on a regular and frequent basis. Part of that learning occurs because the children have a model of reading provided for them, some of it concerned with the simple physical aspects of reading.

How do you hold a book? Which part do you read? Where do you start and finish each page and ultimately the book? Strickland and Morrow (1989) argue that children learn how to handle books by observing adults reading stories. One child alone has greater opportunity to note how the book is handled when a parent reads it but a class of nursery children can also learn from the model of reading provided by an adult. Their learning is helped by the teacher showing the book to the children while it is being read, which she can do because she already knows the story.

So during a story reading the children will see how a book is held and note the front-to-back directionality. The teacher occasionally points to the print while reading, so they also see left-to-right directionality. For example when a nursery teacher read the story of *This is the Bear and the Scary Night* (Hayes, 1991) to a class of three and four year olds, she read the first two pages:

Teacher   *This is the boy*

                     who forgot his bear

                     and left him behind

                     in the park on a chair.

but also showed the pages to the children while running her finger along the line being read. Done once, it might not mean a great deal to the children but over time, with regular and frequent readings of this book and others, children will learn a good deal about reading from such modelling. (Before reading those two pages the teacher had talked with the children about the cover of the book and the first illustration. The children had decided it was a book about a bear, that the bear was sitting on a picnic chair in a park, and that part of the story was about night because they could see the moon – although they first debated whether it was the sun or the moon).

Beyond observing these physical aspects of reading children also acquire a model of story language. They learn not only about new words and how they are brought together into sentences but also about how stories are constructed (Dombey, (1988). In a conventional sense, they learn about the place of such phrases as 'Once upon a time...' and about more complex aspects of story structure. Carol Fox (1993) demonstrates how pre-school children who have heard many stories read to them are able to construct and tell stories which are 'rich and complex' in language.

Even with all the undoubted advantages that story reading provides in terms of handling books and learning about language, it is possible that the children nearest to the teacher have an adavantage because they can see clearly what the teacher is doing. Using big books for a shared book experience allows aspects of reading to be modelled more fully.

Shared book experience

When Don Holdaway (1979) introduced the idea of shared book experience with big books he argued that children needed to have the print in front of them and in a large enough format to 'be seen, shared and discussed'. Accordingly, he constructed big books or large sheets with prominent print, so that all the children in the class could clearly see the print being read. Such shared book experiences are now common in nursery and infant classrooms as a supplement to story readings and specifically to model reading for the children.

Take the example of a nursery teacher sharing *Teddy Bear, Teddy Bear* (Edge, 1988) with a class of twenty-six four year olds:

Teacher   Shall we have a look at this book?

Children   Yes.

Teacher	So what do you think it is about?
Danny	A baby bear.
Teacher	About a baby bear, right.
	How do you know it's going to be about a baby bear?
Danny	'Cos it's little.
Jade	You can see the picture.
Teacher	That's right, the picture, Jade.
	Is there anything else that tells us it might be about a teddy bear?
Georgia	The writing.
Teacher	Where's the writing?
Georgia	At the top of the picture.
Teacher	That's right at the top of the picture.
Rachel	We could colour that in.
Teacher	Yes, we could, couldn't we?
	It says
	Teddy Bear, *(Teacher points to each word*
	Teddy Bear. and reads).

Using the front cover to introduce the book, the teacher encouraged the children to make predictions about the text. The children had evidently looked at other big books, because they could tell where the writing would be and how that would help with the reading. When the teacher read the title of the book she indicated each word as she read it – so providing a very clear model of reading. The teacher then started to read:

Teacher	Shall we start?
Children	Yeah.
Teacher	Right, what do you think the Teddy Bear is doing in this picture?

Leanne	Playing.
Teacher	Playing, yes. Anyone think it is doing something else?
Russell	It's turning around.
Teacher	Good boy. I think Russell might be right, he says it's turning around.

Shall we read what it says?

> *Teddy Bear, Teddy Bear,*
>
> *Turn around.*

You were right Russell, yes.

What is the Teddy Bear doing now, John?

John	Rolling, he's fallen down.
Teacher	He's fallen down. So what is he touching?
Children	The floor.
Teacher	The floor, isn't he? Right.

What will tell me what the Teddy Bear is doing?

Georgia	The writing at the top.
Teacher	Good girl, the writing at the top.

> *Teddy Bear, Teddy Bear,*
>
> *Touch the ground.*

Can you touch the ground, with your hands?

Right, that's what Teddy Bear was doing.

Shall we see what else he's doing?

Children	Yeah.
Teacher	Right, oh what's he doing now?
Leanne	He's hurt his leg.

Teacher   Do you think he's hurt his leg, Leanne? Mmh, perhaps he's doing something else.

Christopher Putting his shoes on.

Teacher   He might be sh...

Georgia   Shaking his shoes.

Teacher   He might be shaking his shoes, he might Georgia.

Billy Joe   No, he's hurt his leg.

Teacher   He's hurt his leg. What will tell me what Teddy Bear is doing?

Jade   The writing.

Teacher   The writing.

> *Teddy Bear, Teddy Bear,*
>
> *Show your shoes.*

He's showing us his shoe.

Can you show me your shoe?

That's lovely, right.

With each of the first three pages the teacher asked the children to predict from the pictures what the bear was doing and what the text might say. Then, as she read each page she followed the print with her finger so that a connection could be made between the print and the reading. Where possible she involved the children further, getting them to 'touch the ground' and 'show your shoe', so linking the text to experience. Furthermore, with each page, she asked different children to indicate what would help convey what the Teddy Bear was doing. The children indicated that the writing would tell about the bear.

Although the teacher was not teaching reading directly, she gave a very clear modelling of reading. She extended it when the book was completed, reading through again but this time inviting the children to join in.

Teacher   Do you want to share it with me again?

Do you want to join in with the writing?

Children   Yeah.

Teacher   So what does it say?

T/Ch   (With the teacher pointing to the words)

Teddy Bear, Teddy Bear,
Turn around.

Teddy Bear, Teddy Bear,

Touch the ground........

During that second reading the teacher and children read through without interruption, the children reading as an echo of the teacher. Her modelling of the reading enabled the children to see and hear the reading of the book, and to act like readers themselves during the joint reading (although most of them were probably not reading in the strictest sense).

The shared book experience allows teachers to model reading but this need not always be centred on a book. Teachers can construct big sheets of nursery rhymes and songs to use with the children and use some of the classroom print.

Shared reading

In addition to story readings and shared book experiences with the whole class or large groups, teachers and other adults can occasionally share a book with an individual child, for instance when an adult visits the library or other setting to look at and read a book. On such occasions it is not uncommon for a child to ask the adult to read the book to them. Or the teacher might notice a child not settling to an activity and suggest a shared reading. Where there is substantial provision of books in an interesting setting and an emphasis upon story reading children are likely to ask adults to read with them.

Shared reading will vary in its nature and format according to the book being read and the level of reading development of the child. Initially, the child might have the story read and comment on the story as it is read. Later, as reading develops, the child will read part of the story to the adult, with support as necessary (Campbell, 1995a). However, whatever the nature of the shared reading, in the early stages and especially the nursery years, the adult will model the reading.

When a teacher shared the book *I wish I could fly* (Maris,1986) with four year old Michael they first had a long discussion about the book (described in the next chapter):

Teacher   Shall I read it to you now?

Michael   Yeah.

Teacher   So what will tell us all about the story?

Michael   The writing.   (Pointing to the words and moving his finger under the words and across the page).

Teacher   The writing. And it says:

> *I wish I could fly.*

So who wishes he could fly?

Michael   The tortoise, but tortoises can't fly.

Teacher   No, tortoises can't fly.

> *Good morning, Bird.*
>
> *I wish I could fly like you.*

So, even though they had a prior discussion of the book, the reading was still punctuated by comments by both participants. Nevertheless, the teacher provided a model of the reading and Michael, sitting beside her in the library corner, followed it. Michael demonstrated both verbally and physically that he had awareness of writing and reading:

Michael   The writing.   (Pointing to the words and moving his finger under the words and across the page).

His awareness should ensure that he could learn more about reading as the teacher read the story, helped by his close proximity to the teacher and the book, and by having individual attention.

Michael's degree of attention to the book is apparent at the point when the teacher reaches the end of the story:

Teacher   *"...when it rains, I don't get wet, I'm*

                 Snug, Warm, Cosy and Dry."

Michael   That's why he's in his shell.

Teacher   Is he happy now?

Michael   (Nods).

Teacher   So what can he do?

Michael   He can only duck in his shell – so can those two snails.

Although Michael had apparently not seen this book before, he spotted the two snails in their shells in the final illustration. He might have paid more attention to the illustrations than the print but his comments show how in a one-to-one shared reading the child is well placed to note the detailed features on each page.

The children's attention will also be focused on the print at times, and this enables them to make links with the reading modelled by the teacher. Teachers and parents will know how, once children have had a story modelled for them, future readings have to conform to that model. A single word missed or out of place can evoke a comment. And it is not uncommon for a child to ask: 'Where does it say morning?' Michael observed that: 'My name is like morning.' associating with the letter 'm'. These are some of the gains of providing a model of reading during teacher-child shared readings.

Writing

Earlier we mentioned that some children might already have helped parents to construct shopping lists and seen adults compile lists of items to be purchased. From observations of that model, children will set out to construct a list of items to be bought. We soon recognise that it is a shopping list because it will be set out with short scribbles one below another, even if each item is unreadable. In the nursery classroom we want to build upon such beginnings or provide similar models of writing for other children.

From observations in one nursery classroom, Margaret Lally (1991) described how the nursery teacher worked together with the children to produce some print for the classroom. The print was being produced for a real purpose. The teacher constructed a written notice, with guidance from the children, to remind parents to close the latch on the nursery gate, thus modelling writing for the children. As we might expect, many other notices were produced by the three and four year olds during the next few days, as they imitated the behaviour of the teacher and explored other opportunities for making notices.

Opportunities arise for adults in the nursery classroom to create classroom print with children. Notices can be written for a wide variety of purposes e.g. forthcoming events and a few carefully selected labels can be used in the classroom to indicate for instance where materials such as pencils or paper are kept. However, notices and labels will be virtually useless to children of this age, unless the children are involved in generating them and help in the modelling of the print. Subsequently the adults will need to talk with the children about these notices.

The teacher can also model writing, with a group or the whole class, as a means of talking about nursery rhymes. First she writes the nursery rhyme with the children's support. These written rhymes in big print and on big sheets are useful as part of shared reading experiences. Encouraging the children to take part in making the nursery sheets leads to dialogue which suggests that the children are leading in the construction of the rhymes and the teacher is following their instructions:

Teacher   So if I write

           Humpty Dumpty

           Now, what comes next?

Children   *sat on a wall*

Teacher   I'll write

sat on a ...

Children	*wall*
Teacher	*wall.*

During such a process the children see the words formed before them, letter by letter, as the teacher writes and speaks the word at the same time. The process of modelling writing is extended when the teacher uses the written rhyme to model reading. This later modelling of reading is enhanced by the fact that the children have been involved in the construction of the reading matter.

Writing can be modelled even more informally when adults visit the play area or writing centre. For instance, when, as we have noted, a telephone is provided in the play area with a message pad and pencil beside it. Modelling message writing can stimulute children to write while engaged in imaginative play. Adults can join in with the writing, describing the words as they are written. Such modelling of writing can support the children's growing understanding of literacy.

After a visit or outing, children and teacher can work together to produce some writing, with the teacher modelling the children's suggestions. An organised walk will elicit comments by the children and these can be brought together by the teacher in a collective story or statement about such activities, as here:

Teacher	So, what shall we tell about our walk?
John	We saw a hedgehog.
Russell	It was dead.
Teacher	So, shall I write about the hedgehog?
Children	Yeah.
Teacher	Should I say – On our walk, first?
Rachel	*We went for a walk.*
Teacher	Okay.
	We went ...

Such collective writing, not unlike a language experience approach (Goddard, 1974), helps children to be party to the construction of the writing and to watch as the teacher models it for them. But it is not the modelling of literacy alone which helps children to construct a sense of literacy. Children have to explore literacy for themselves, especially along-side adults in interactions related to literacy. It is those interactions to which we now turn.

Chapter 5

Interacting with literacy

As the foregoing accounts show, modelling literacy is not an isolated activity. Typically, the adult models reading or writing as part of an interaction with a child, group or class. In the shared book experience with *Teddy Bear, Teddy Bear* the modelling was a key aspect of a larger interaction.

Such interactions are an important part of literacy learning. Margaret Clark (1976) suggests that story readings were an important feature in the lives of children who became young fluent readers but that also important was an interested adult taking time to answer the child's questions. When children can share the literacy experience with an adult, ask questions, discuss aspects of print, talk about stories and relate the context to their own experiences, they are being enabled to learn about reading and writing and to read and write (Smith, 1978).

We need, therefore, to look again briefly at some literacy activities used by nursery teachers and nurses in the classroom so as to examine its interactive nature.

Story reading

We have already noted the value of story readings and the adult's role and considered the modelling of literacy offered by story readings. Attention was drawn to their interactive nature and how a class of three and four year olds will try to participate in the story reading by making comments relating the story to their own experiences, making predictions and interpreting objects or events. This is especially true when adults recognise the importance of encouraging the children to participate actively. Dombey (1988) illustrates how nursery classroom story readings can be interactive occasions for encouraging children towards literacy.

In the account of the teacher modelling the first two pages of *This is the Bear and the Scary Night* (Hayes, 1991) with a class of three and four year olds, the interactive nature of the activity was exemplified:

Teacher   *This is the bear*

              up in the sky.

Georgia   The owl's taken him away.

Dean   He's got the Teddy Bear.

Teacher   He has.

Georgia   'Cos he's got sharp nails.

Teacher   *This is the owl*

              who struggled to fly.

Ben   I thought that was the sun.

Teacher   It's not though, is it?

Children   No.

Ben   It's the moon.

Teacher   Mmh.

Jamie   He's going to the owl's tree.

Teacher   He might do, yes.

Even in this short extract the children can be observed making comments about characters and objects in the story: 'I thought that was the sun'; providing an interpretation of an event: 'Cos he's got sharp nails' and predicting an outcome to an event: 'He's going to the owl's tree'. We can also observe the teacher's responses and encouragement.

Reading stories in this way to young children provides the opportunity for the children to create their own sense of order and meaning about the story. Their involvement with the language and structure of stories will support their literacy learning.

Shared book experience

Modelling reading is only one feature of a shared book experience. We saw how the teacher also encouraged the children to be involved actively in the reading – for instance by showing their shoes, just like Teddy Bear; predicting what might happen; and by reminding the teacher that what Teddy Bear was now doing would be revealed in the text.

Here is another short section of the shared book experience centred on the book *Teddy Bear, Teddy Bear*:

Teacher   Oh, what do you think the Teddy Bear's doing now?

Michael   Shut one eye.

Teacher   What do we say when we shut one eye?

Michael   Wink.

Teacher   Winking, right.

Michael   I can wink.

Teacher   Can you all wink?

Danny   I can, yeah.

Teacher   Oh, you are showing me beautifully.

The teacher asks the children to consider the next picture and predict what the text might be about. And having established that the Bear was closing one eye, she was able to get the children to give the precise term 'wink' and further involved them with the text by encouraging them to wink.

When the teacher moved the conversation from winking it was to ask about the writing. She provided numerous comments to help her class understand the nature of reading:

Teacher   What shall I do now (points to the print)?

Georgia   Read the writing.

Teacher   Good girl, Georgia, I'm going to read the writing.

> *Teddy Bear, Teddy Bear,*
>
> *Wink one eye.*

Oh, you are doing it beautifully, yes.

Danny   I can.

Teacher   And what's Teddy Bear going to do now?

Children   Cry.

Teacher   Oh, he's going to cry.

> *Teddy Bear, Teddy Bear,*
>
> *Start to cry.*

Bradley   What's he crying for?

Billy Joe   What's wrong with him?

Teacher   Well, I wonder what's wrong with him? What do you think could be wrong with him?

Billy   He's hungry.

Nikki   His mummy's gone.

Teacher   His mummy's gone or he could be hungry. Perhaps you were right Billy, he's hungry. Anything else why he could be crying?

Russell   A dirty nappy.

Bradley   He's lost.

Jade   Let's read it.

Teacher   Oh, you want me to read it.

After reading the page where Teddy Bear starts to cry, one of the children asked: 'What's he crying for?' and the range of responses indicated their wide range of experience and their ability to empathise with Teddy. But it was Jade who recognised that the guessing might best be resolved by reading the text.

The shared book experience allows the children to learn from the teacher and from each other; about the book being read and about some aspects of the nature of print. The teacher is not teaching directly about reading but she is enabling the children to share the book with her in an enjoyable way and is thus encouraging learning.

Shared reading

Story readings and shared book experiences provide opportunities for the children to enjoy stories and books, to have the reading modelled for them, to think about the text and to make predictions in a group or whole class. In contrast, shared readings are organised in a nursery classroom to allow children to interact with an adult on a one-to-one basis. In a sense they are special, because the teacher is able to vary the experience to suit the interests and needs of the individual child. She can to some extent determine from the responses what learning is taking place and adopt her strategies and comments accordingly. Additionally, and importantly, the shared reading can give the child an enjoyable contact with books.

We know from the earlier chapter that teachers will often model the reading of the book during a shared reading. When the child is older and has more experience with literacy, the shared reading gives the child a chance to read some of the book alone – but supported by the adult. However, in the nursery classroom it is more likely that the shared reading will concentrate upon a conversation about the book, as described below in Michael's sharing of *I wish I could fly* with his teacher. This shared reading started with them discussing the book as they looked at the pictures together:

Teacher   What do you think the tortoise is doing?

Michael   He's jumping.

Teacher   He's jumping, yes.

The cover of the book does give the impression of the tortoise jumping, or attempting to fly.

Michael and his teacher then begin to look through the book together. Michael appears to be used to such interactions, immediately taking a leading role, talking about the pictures and so about the story:

Teacher   Shall we look at the pictures to see what he's doing?

Michael   First – first he's gone down his home.

Teacher   He has, he's tucked into his home, hasn't he?

             Who's looking at him?

Michael   That bird. He's looking down at him.

Teacher   He is indeed. Now, what is he trying to do?

Michael   He's trying to flap his wings and fly off.

Teacher   What about the tortoise?

Michael   He's got his head.

Michael's observations about the tortoise pulling its head in and out of its shell accurately reflected the initial pictures. His comments that the bird was 'trying to flap his wings and fly off' are a good interpretation of the illustrations and suggest that he has a good oral vocabulary.

The fact that the tortoise has its mouth open and that there is some speech on the page probably led the teacher to ask:

Teacher   Do you think he's talking?

Michael   That might say he's talking. (Pointing to the writing).

Teacher   I wonder what that is?

Michael   It's a word.

Teacher	It is some words, it says:

Good morning, Bird.

Michael	And there's some bees on that picture.
Teacher	Yes.
Michael	And then he jumps.
Teacher	He does.
Michael	And there's a little frog and some snails.

Michael's responses indicated that he had a developing knowledge about print and some of the language that describes it. He then moved on to talk about features of the illustrations (although his 'bees' were actually dragonflies) whereupon it became Michael who led the interaction and decided what to talk about.

The shared reading continued, the teacher and Michael looking at and talking about the book. The teacher modelled the reading but there was also conversation. This allowed the child to talk about the book, make predictions and share with the teacher in determining what is important. These processes all contribute to the child's development towards conventional reading.

Writing

In the chapter on modelling literacy we considered two instances where the class or group of children were able to contribute to the teacher's modelling of writing even though the contribution consisted mainly of providing or saying the words for the teacher to write. Later, the children might be able to participate more actively in the writing.

On both occasions the teacher did the writing but she did so in discussion with the children about the content. Such interactions around writing help the children learn about print. The two examples, *Humpty Dumpty* and the report of a walk that the children had participated in are indicative of the many opportunities teachers have for demonstrating writing in front of children. Nursery rhymes and songs, children's experiences and the experiences offered by the teacher are rich sources of opportunity for writing. It is important that children are able to play a part in the writing by making comments and suggestions and reminding the teacher about the sequence of words.

These are examples of rather formally organised events designed to enable children to think about literacy, talk with others and share with their teacher. Other more spontaneous occasions can allow teachers to spend a few moments with individual children to consider writing, such as when children write their name or some writing during a play activity at the writing centre.

In the introduction we noted the study by Judith Shickedanz (1990) of the writing development of her son, Adam, and the amount of time that Adam was prepared to spend experimenting with and exploring the letter shapes and sounds making up his name. His explorations appeared to begin with a drawing at the age of two years and eight months which contained an approximation to an 'A'. Within a year, in which he made many experiments with letters, Adam was writing his name. Another study by Harste, Woodward and Burke (1984), also demonstrates that children are intrigued to find out about their own name and to represent it on paper. They describe how the teacher in one class of three year olds initiated a 'sign-in' activity and how it encouraged the children to record daily their own attendance in the classroom. This seems a bold activity for a nursery classroom and no doubt some of the children would produce just a scribble and others possibly one letter of their forename (typically the first), while only an exceptional few would get closer to writing their own names. Nevertheless, a 'sign-in' activity can stimulate a good deal of interest among children for a while. Teachers can devise other opportunities for children to experiment with name writing so as to encourage writing in general and they should be prepared for the children's questions about name writing:

David   How do you write a D?

Teacher   (Writes D)

           There you are.

David   I've got two.

Teacher   What? Two D's.

David   Yeah.

Teacher   Where are the two D's?

David   In – in my name.

Teacher   That's right, you have.

The progress of each child towards writing his/her name cannot be rushed, but teachers do need to provide opportunities for them to experiment and be prepared to participate in interactions with them about their forenames.

Not all the writing that nursery children attempt will be in relation to their own name. Certain play activities might stimulate children to try to write, especially if the nursery teacher or other adult in the classroom has informally demonstrated the possibilities for writing possibly in the ways we noted earlier, with telephone messages.

Teacher   Is that the telephoning ringing?

          Hello.

          You're going to come later, I'll make a note of that.

          (Writes in message pad)

          John will come at 2 o'clock.

Anne   I need to talk on the telephone.

Teacher   All right, here you are.

Anne   Hello.

          Can you come to tea?

          (Scribbles some vertical lines on to the pad)

Her scribbling of vertical lines will develop towards more conventional letters and print as writing is modelled elsewhere and at other times in the classroom, and as she has frequent chances to write for herself.

A writing centre in the classroom creates opportunities for children to write regularly and frequently and in various formats. At times they might visit it to write their names or perhaps about a picture they have drawn or painted. At other times they might watch an adult writing in the centre and then produce similar writing themselves:

Teacher   I'd better make my shopping list.

Now let me see.

Tea.

Butter.

Milk.

Cornflakes.

Soap.

That's what I'll need tonight.

Ben   I go shopping with my mummy.

Teacher   Do you?

Ben   Yeah.

Teacher   Do you take a shopping list with you?

Ben   I – I can do it.

(Writes in a column format with lines and circles.)

Teacher   So what are you getting?

Ben   Sweets and bananas and biscuits and – and coffee.

Such interactions around writing might almost be contagious. Once they take place the writing of lists can become a major activity for a few days. When children play out the various roles involved in shopping they are likely to produce numerous lists or what look like lists for their shopping.

Children like to explore writing and are helped if the adults around them model writing for them and, importantly, talk to them about writing. During interactions of this kind children observe writing and are supported in their developing understanding of writing by the comments and questions of the adult.

Chapter 6

Using nursery rhymes and songs

Adults frequently use nursery rhymes and songs in the nursery classroom because of the shared enjoyment that can be derived from them. Dorothy White (1954) observed that her daughter, Carol, demonstrated a love of rhyme and rhythm in language. When Carol was three years old she would 'talk the rhymes over to herself' (p.55) as she looked through a book of rhymes. Children enjoy the play with language in nursery rhymes, songs and also in finger plays:

> *Round and round the garden*
>
> *went the Teddy Bear*
>
> *one step*
>
> *two steps*
>
> *tickly under there.*

This is one that children might have encountered before starting at the nursery and there are numerous others (e.g. Matterson's collection (1969) includes finger games as well as nursery rhymes).

Furthermore, observations of young children physically engaged in games and activities show that some are associated with rhymes and stories. Iona and Peter Opie (1959) have provided us with details of hundreds of such rhymes including the topical:

> *Mickey Mouse came into my house,*
>
> *I asked him what he wanted.*
>
> *A piece an' jam*
>
> *A slice of ham*
>
> *And that was all he wanted.* (p111)

Children enjoy chanting such rhymes as they play with the language handed down from earlier generations of children. Barrie Wade (1990) notes the extensive use of rhymes during jumping, skipping and clapping games. He suggests that the rhymes contribute to children's concept of story as well as to their pleasure in language itself. So such rhymes should be part of nursery classroom routines.

As nursery teachers will know, finger plays and nursery rhymes can be used to bring the class together, perhaps towards the end of the morning or afternoon. They serve, therefore, a practical and useful function. The teacher and children in one nursery classroom were observed singing as the class came together at the end of, a period of self-directed activities, for a story reading:

> *One, two, three, four, five,*
>
> *once I caught a fish alive.*
>
> *Six, seven, eight, nine, ten,*
>
> *then I let it go again.*
>
> *Why did you let it go?*
>
> *Because it bit my finger so.*
>
> *Which finger did it bite?*
>
> *This little finger on the right.*

This rhyme has rhyming elements and also counting, using the fingers, allowing children to learn about their five fingers on each hand and possibly about left and right, as they wiggle the 'little finger on the right'. Although the rhymes can be used to facilitate transitions they are too valuable to be used solely for this purpose. Finger plays, nursery rhymes, songs and poems are working forms of language activity in their own right.

The evidence from classrooms shows that children soon acquire a repertoire of known rhymes from such language activities, in some cases building on the repertoire that they bring from home. Knowledge of such rhymes and the ability to present them in unison – which in itself, according to Holdaway (1979) has a social benefit – will encourage children to act out the rhymes in their play and to represent them in their drawings and paintings. Such enthusiasm for the rhymes can be channelled by the teacher into the production of large pictorial wall friezes around a chosen rhyme allowing for modelling the writing of it.

This writing can be used subsequently with the children to model the reading of it. The teacher can read the rhyme to the children or with them, pointing to certain words as it is read. The frieze and the choral reading of it can be used as a focal point at the start or end of the day when the children come together.

In the chapter on modelling literacy, we noted the written modelling of a nursery rhyme, as the children and teacher together constructed the rhyme:

Teacher   So if I write

        Humpty Dumpty

        Now, what comes next?

Children   *sat on a wall*

Teacher   I'll write

        sat on a ...

Children   *wall*

Teacher   *wall.*

Here the teacher was indeed modelling the writing, and in reponse to the children's instructions. But additionally, in order to confirm what she had just written, she had the chance to model the reading of each sentence before continuing with her writing:

Teacher   There we are.

>   *Humpty Dumpty*

T/Ch   *sat on a wall.*

Teacher   Now

>   *Humpty*

Children   *Dumpty*

>   *had a great fall.*

While constructing familiar nursery rhymes teachers can try to elicit individual contributions from children but the interaction will flow more naturally if their contributions are accepted in unison. Children know certain rhymes so well that they will recite them at once and teachers may have to slow them down to produce the writing.

Once a nursery rhyme has been written on a large sheet it can be used in the same way as big books to provide a model of reading. Involving children with rhyming elements such as 'wall' and 'fall' helps them towards an understanding of phonology, thus contributing towards their reading development. Margaret Meek (1990) advises: 'Please teach children nursery rhymes, and the phonology will come, noticed with fun' (p151). She takes account of the important work of Kornei Chukovsky (1963) on children's fascination with rhyming words and their pleasure in rhyme. Chukovsky quotes his four-year-old son's rhyming poem:

>   *I'm a big, big rider,*

>   *You're smaller than a spider.* (p64)

Meek believes that we need to teach rhymes because they are a valuable source of language that has survived over the ages and been handed down as part of popular culture. The learning of phonology is indeed incidental.

If rhymes were to be taught to assure reading development the magic might well vanish and the sheer enjoyment of playing with rhyming language be lost.

The link between using and learning nursery rhymes and developing as a reader has been established also in psychological studies (e.g. Goswami and Bryant, 1990). Bryant's studies with young children indicate that children with a knowledge of nursery rhymes at three years of age are well placed to acquire phonemic awareness within the next year and to be reading and spelling at six. A phonemic awareness suggests that the children would have acquired an awareness of letter sounds but, perhaps more importantly, they will have developed an awareness of onset and rime. The link between onset and rime and nursery rhymes is easy to identify and can be made explicit: in Humpty Dumpty the rhyme is created by 'wall' and 'fall' which have an onset 'w' and 'f' (the opening phonological unit) and a rime element 'all' (the closing phonological unit).

Young children who have frequent opportunities to enjoy rhymes soon recognise the onset and rime elements in the language – although, of course, they are not able to talk about it explicitly. They also like to play with language themselves and create their own rhymes (Dowker, 1989). Three year old Afua, for instance, made up a poem which included a rhyme where onset and rime were demonstrated as a central feature:

The bird does jump,

mump and dump. (p189)

Here, in the first two lines of what Dowker calls a line chant, the rhyming element arguably takes precedence over meaning.

We need, then, to use finger games, nursery rhymes, songs and poems with children in the nursery classroom. Play with language is an important part of their cultural heritage and their learning. Furthermore, it contributes to the children's awareness of language, their knowledge and phonological awareness of onset and rime and their later reading development. All this happens when adults and children share the enjoyment of the various rhymes during the course of the day, emphasing the fun and the language possibilities created by the rhymes and the children's use of them.

Chapter 7

Talking about environmental and classroom print

We noted earlier how talking about environmental and classroom print might have beneficial effects upon children's literacy development. Even before beginning nursery schooling, children will be surrounded by environmental print and will try to make sense of some of it. We noted how Zachary talked with his parents about it (Laminack, 1991) and other studies also record how children ask about the print they encounter in the environment (e.g. Baghban, 1984). Adults in the nursery classroom can build upon this curiousity and interest, providing opportunities for involvement with print to encourage meaningful engagements with literacy. We also saw how, in relation to modelling literacy, classroom print can be developed for real purposes, like notices to close the gate (Lally, 1991). When the teacher uses this print to talk about it and its purpose with the children it can encourage them to think about print and to write.

Nursery teachers can do a good deal to encourage talk about environmental print. One nursery teacher had ended a day by reading the story of Goldilocks and the Three Bears and next day she prepared porridge in the classroom, so that it greeted the children when they entered the room, bubbling in a pan (protected by another adult). This caused great excitement and talk. But before the children could sample the porridge they were taken for a walk by the teacher – just like the three bears – so that the porridge could cool.

Back in the classroom, the children tried the porridge for themselves with milk or without, with or without sugar or salt. For most of the children it was the first time that they had seen or tasted porridge, and some were reluctant to try it. The teacher had anticipated this reluctance so she also brought in a dozen small cereal boxes as alternatives. And she used these to ask the children about their knowledge of environmental print:

Teacher   Who can pick out what they had for breakfast?

Samantha Cornflakes.

Teacher   Can you go and take the cornflakes packet?

Samantha This one.

Teacher   How do you know it is the cornflakes?

Samantha 'Cos I do.

Teacher   Why?

Samantha 'Cos it's got a chicken.

Teacher   Mmh, anything else.

Samantha The writing says cornflakes.

Teacher   That's right.

           That says cornflakes, doesn't it.

Samantha And you can see the picture.

Teacher   Yes, you can.

We cannot tell what enabled Samantha to select the cornflakes. She did mention the writing so it may have been significant – or did she know that her teacher would welcome such a response? However, she also mentioned two other features of the packet: the chicken and the picture, by which we might infer that she means the representation of cornflakes on the packet. Whatever the key feature, Samantha, like others in the class, was able to select the appropriate box.

It is interesting to note the comments from two other children:

Jamie   I had CocoPops.

Teacher   Have we got that one here?

Jamie   Yeah.

Teacher   Which one is it.

Jamie   That one. (Jamie picks it out).

Teacher   How do you know?

Jamie   Because of the writing and the brown picture.

Sam   I like Rice Krispies.

Teacher   Which is the Rice Krispie box?

Sam   The one with the funny men on. (Sam takes the packet).

Teacher   Yes, it's got Snap, Crackle and Pop, hasn't it?

Sam   And you can see the writing.

Teacher   That's right, it says Rice Krispies.

Both Jamie and Sam selected the correct boxes of cereal and both mentioned two features of the boxes. They noted, respectively, the writing and a dominant colour, and the writing and the three characters. It might have been the colours and the characters which were the real key but both children were aware that the writing could also be helpful, whether they used it or not. It would appear that they were developing an awareness of the functional uses of print.

With such time and energy devoted to environmental print it is not surprising that the following morning one of the children should want to tell the teacher about a shopping expedition with a parent:

Michael   I went to Sainsbury shopping.

Teacher   Did you?

Michael   Yeah, I got some cornflakes for my mum, the little ones.

Teacher   How did you know to get the cornflakes?

Michael   'Cos the writing.

Teacher   That's right, and anything else?

Michael   Yeah, the cockerel. I helped my mum with the cornflakes.

Teacher   Good boy, well done, Michael.

Once again it was the writing and a key character the child noted as his guide to recognition. Michael's mention of shopping could lead to a group or class discussion about it and that, in turn, can lead to setting up a shop, or replica supermarket, in the play area/home corner. A shop allows for numerous examples of environmental print to be introduced into the nursery classroom and can be the basis for a good deal of imaginative play – including encouraging the writing of shopping lists.

Linda Miller (1995) describes how setting up a shop encouraged a good deal of activity from the children in one nursery classroom and their substantial involvement with environmental print. The adults then helped the children to make books containing the cut-and-paste logos from various packets. These books were talked about and read with parents. Some of the cut-out logos were mounted onto card for the children to play games of Snap. Such matching games require children to look carefully and identify the various logos. So environmental print can be used to good purpose in a classroom shop and can lead to other literacy activities. And, as noted in chapter two, other settings eg. the dentist's, or a garage will also encourage the provision of a range of environmental print.

As well as providing this print, adults need to be in the shop at times to support the children in their discussions about print. Using the environmental print, talking about it and modelling its possible uses are all required from the adults in the nursery classroom.

...dren should learn from everything that happens to them and
...n; they do not separate their learning into different subjects
...es.

...arn most effectively through actions rather than instruction.

...arn best when they are actively involved and interested.

...ho feel confident in themselves and their own ability have a
...o learning.

...eed time and space to produce work of quality and depth.

...dren can do (rather than what they cannot do) is the starting
...eir learning.

...onversation are the main ways by which young children learn
...mselves, other people and the world around them.

...who are encouraged to think for themselves are more likely to
...endently.

...tionships which children make with other children and with
...e of central importance to their development. (pp51-53).

...der some of the links between these principles and the literacy
...he present book.

...g emerging literacy prepares the children for the literacy
...later life and equally importantly, helps children come to terms
...int environment in which they live. When teachers provide
...s for engaging with print children are enabled to answer
...hich are of importance to them at the time (1). Literacy activities
...y reading satisfy children intellectually and support their literacy
...the same time the social setting of the reading responds to their
...moral and spiritual needs – growth is indeed interwoven (2).
...brings to the nursery classroom different levels of understanding
...cy and different abilities to deal with it. The concept of emerging
...ognises this, and the teacher supports children in whatever aspect
...is currently important or interesting to them (3 and 9). This book
...eracy as part of the nursery classroom day; literacy is not isolated

Other classroom print can also be added. And, as noted earlier (Lally, 1991), once teacher and children start to talk about notices and labels the children are very likely to take on the task of themselves producing some print for the play area or the classroom. Whoever produces classroom print, there is still the need to ensure that it is talked about and that adults guide children to appreciate the message provided on notices or labels.

As well as a favourite nursery rhyme being printed on a large sheet and put on a classroom wall children's drawings and paintings can be used to surround and highlight the print. Children can be reminded of the nursery rhyme from time to time and teachers can use it to engage children in the rhyme and to model a reading of the print.

The possibilities for classroom print in early years classrooms are vast. For instance, some 'road signs' were placed at a low level around one nursery classroom. The signs had pictures in the middle of a red circle and a message written outside the circle. Because they were so constructed, there was a link with environmental print with which the children would be familiar from their observations of road signs. However, the classroom 'road signs' were actually indicating classroom rules and expectations 'Be kind and caring', 'Walk nicely' etc., and could be used to remind children about classroom behaviour.

Teachers can use their knowledge of the locality of the school and their awareness of the interests of the children to develop various forms of classroom print and should be sure to include the children's given name/ forenames. Many children arrive at the nursery classroom with some simple understanding of their names. So, when three year old Max found an 'alphabetti spaghetti' shape and said 'This is an x' (Miller, 1995) he could recognise it, label it and knew it as one of the letters from his name.

We saw how much time and energy Adam devoted to writing, particularly his own name. Adam developed from writing the letter 'A' to producing his complete name, around his third birthday (Shickedanz, 1990). This involvement with one's name led Harste et al (1984) to suggest the 'sign-in' activity for three year olds. The use of children's names and other forms of classroom print encourages children to engage with print and it provides an important focus for adults and children to talk about literacy.

4) Young ch
around th
or discipl

5) Children

6) Children

7) Children
headsta

8) Childre

9) What
point i

Chapter

Conclusi

This book has explored emergent literacy
classroom and the provision, activities and
Concentration upon a specific area is import
and content of this crucial part of the curricu
the context of nursery education in general.

Christopher Ball (1994) in a report for the
mental principles for good practice in pre-sch

1) Early childhood is the foundation on whi
their lives. But it is not just a preparation
hood: it has an importance in itself.

2) Children develop at different rates, and in d
intellectually, morally, socially, physically
portant; each is interwoven with others.

3) All children have abilities which can (and
promoted.

10) Play a
about

11) Child
act ir

12) The
adul

Let us c
practice

Encour
deman
with t
opport
questi
such a
grow
emot
Each
abou
liter
of li
pres

from other activities nor learnt as a separate subject. Rather, it is part of the school day and integrates reading and writing for a real purpose with a wide range of other curriculum areas (4). Writing at the writing centre, joining in with nursery rhymes, engaging with literacy in the play area, and contributing to teachers' story readings ensures that children are involved with and interested in literacy. It is this involvement that fosters the emergence of literacy rather than direct instruction (5 and 6). When children are encouraged to write at the writing centre and during play, and to contribute to readings during story readings, shared book experience and shared reading, they develop a confidence in their abilities as readers and writers which helps in subsequent learning (7). These processes cannot be rushed and the adults in the nursery classroom need to ensure that time and space are available, as well as materials, to provide for a depth of learning (8). Provision of this kind encourages the children to play at literacy and to develop confidence that they can do much of it independently or alongside their peers (10 and 11). This book acknowledges the central importance of adults, as the ones who provide, read, model, interact, use and talk about reading and writing in order to support children's literacy (10 and 12).

So how might the nursery classroom look at any given moment? Groups of children may be playing with sand, using building blocks, or painting, while others are supported by an adult on a group task and still others are engaged in socio-dramatic play in the play area. A few children may be at the writing centre and one or two on the floor, on a cushion or a chair in the library corner looking at or reading books, leading perhaps to a shared reading with an adult.

Outside children may be involved with larger materials and apparatus in solitary imaginative play or with others in socially agreed play. Children may be painting or writing at an easel. The adults move between the various activities, supporting children with literacy and their other learning. Occasionally, usually at the start or end of the session, the class come together for a story reading, shared book experience, or to sing nursery rhymes. So a whole range of activities will be going on, of which literacy is just one important part.

Encouraging literacy learning in the nursery classroom will, for many children, be the logical extension of earlier encouragement at home. Geekie and Raban (1993) suggest that 'interactions between teacher and child should more closely approximate interactions between mothers and their pre-school children' (p12), where the adult facilitates the child's learning in a collaborative construction of meaning. This means providing materials from which children can choose freely and receive adult support as needed.

Opportunities for literacy learning should be as readily available for children in the nursery classroom as they were earlier in the home. The nursery classroom is a natural extension of the home, and should provide an environment in which emerging literacy can be facilitated.

References

Baghban, M. (1984) *Our Daughter Learns to Read and Write.* Newark, Delaware: International Reading Association

Ball, C. (1994) *Start Right: The importance of early learning.* London: RSA

Bissex, G. (1980) *Gnys at Wrk: A Child Learns to Read and Write.* Cambridge, Mass: Harvard University Press

Cambourne, B. (1988) *The Whole Story: Natural Learning and the Acquisition of Literacy in the Classroom.* Auckland: Ashton Scholastic

Campbell, R. (1992) *Reading Real Books.* Buckingham: Open University Press

Campbell, R. (1995a) *Reading in the Early Years: Handbook.* Buckingham: Open University Press

Campbell, R. (1995b) A writing centre in a nursery classroom. *Early Years.* 16, 1. pp9-13

Chukovsky, K. (1963) *From Two to Five.* Berkeley: University of California Press

Clark, M. M. (1976) *Young Fluent Readers.* London: Heinemann Educational

Dombey, H. (1988) Partners in the telling. In M. Meek and C. Mills (Eds) *Language and Literacy in the Primary School.* Lewes: The Falmer Press

Dowker, A. (1989) Rhymes and alliteration in poems elicited from young children. *Journal of Child Language.* 16. pp181-202

Downing, J and Thackray, D. V. (1971) *Reading Readiness.* London: University of London Press

Fox, C. (1993) *At the Very Edge of the Forest: The Influence of Literature on Storytelling by Children.* London: Cassell

Geekie, P. and Raban, B. (1993) *Learning to Read and Write Through Classroom Talk.* Stoke-on-Trent: Trentham Books

Goddard, N. (1974) *Literacy: Language Experience Approach.* London: Macmillan Educational

Goodman, Y. (Ed) (1990) *How Children Construct Literacy.* Newark, Delaware: International Reading Association

Goswami, U. C. and Bryant, P. (1990) *Phonological Skills and Learning to Read.* Hove: Lawrence Erlbaum Associates

Graves, D. (1983) *Writing: Teachers and Children at Work.* Portsmouth, New Hampshire: Heinemann Educational

Hall, N. (1987) *The Emergence of Literacy.* Sevenoaks, Kent: Hodder and Stoughton

Hall, N. and Abbott, L. (Eds) (1991) *Play in the Primary Curriculum.* London: Hodder and Stoughton

Harste, J. C., Woodward, V. A. and Burke, C. L. (1984) *Language Stories & Literacy Lessons.* Portsmouth, New Hampshire: Heinemann Educational Books

HMI (1991) *The Teaching and Learning of Reading in Primary Schools.* London: DES

Holdaway, D. (1979) *The Foundations of Literacy.* London:Ashton Scholastic

Lalley, M. (1991) *The Nursery Teacher in Action.* London: Paul Chapman

Laminck, L. (1991) *Learning with Zachary.* Richmond Hill, Ontario: Scholastic

Manning, K. and Sharp, A. (1977) *Structuring Play in the early years at school.* London: Ward Lock Educational

Matterson, E. (1969) *This Little Puffin ... Finger Plays and Nursery Games.* London: Puffin Books

Meek, M. (1988) *How Texts Teach What Readers Learn.* Stroud: Thimble Press

Meek, M. (1990) What do we know about reading that helps us to teach? In R. Carter (Ed) (1990) *Knowledge about Language and the Curriculum.* London: Hodder & Stoughton

Miller, L. (1995) *Towards Reading: Literacy Development in the Pre-School Years.* Buckingham: Open University Press

Morrow, L. M. (1989) Designing the classroom to promote literacy development. In D. S. Strickland and L. M. Morrow (1989) (Eds) *Emerging Literacy: Young Children Learn to Read and Write.* Newark, Delaware: International Reading Association

Morrow, L. M. and Rand, M. K. (1991) Promoting literacy during play by designing early childhood classroom environments. *The Reading Teacher.* 44, 6. pp 396-402

NCE (1993) *Learning to Suceed: Report of the Paul Hamlyn Foundation.* National Commission on Education. London: Heinemann

Opie, I. and Opie, P. (1959) *The Lore and Language of School Children.* Oxford: Oxford University Press

SCDC (1989) *Becoming a writer: The National Writing Project.* Walton-on-Thames: Nelson

Schickedanz, J. A. (1990) *Adam's Righting Revolutions.* Portsmouth, New Hampshire: Heinemann Educational

Smith, F. (1978) *Reading.* Cambridge: Cambridge University Press.

Spreadbury, J. (1994) *Read Me A Story.* Carlton, Victoria: Australian Reading Association

Strickland, D. S. and Morrow, L. M. (Eds) (1989) *Emerging Literacy: Young Children Learn to Read and Write.* Newark, Delaware: International Reading Association

Taylor, D. (1983) *Family Literacy: Young Children Learning to Read and Write.* Portsmouth, New Hampshire: Heinemann Educational Books

Taylor, D. and Strickland, D. (1986) *Family Storybook Reading.* London: Scholastic

Teale, W. (1984) Reading to Young Children: Its significance for literacy development. In H. Goelman, A. Oberg, and F. Smith. (1984) *Awakening to Literacy.* London: Heinemann Educational Books

Temple, C., Nathan, R., Temple, F. and Burris, N. A. (1988) *The Beginnings of Writing.* London: Allyn and Bacon

Trelease, J. (1989) 2nd revised edition. *The New Read-Aloud Handbook.* London: Penguin Books

Wade, B. (1990) (Ed) *Reading for Real.* Buckingham: Open University Press

Wells, G. (1986) *The Meaning Makers: Children Learning Language and Using Language to Learn.* London: Hodder and Stoughton

White, D. (1954) (1984 edition) *Books before Five.* Portsmouth, New Hampshire: Heinemann

Children's Books

Carle, E. (1969) *The Very Hungry Caterpillar.* New York: Philomel Books

Edge, N. (1988) *Teddy Bear, Teddy Bear.* Salem, Oregon: Resources for Creative Teaching

Hayes, S. (1991) *This is the Bear and the Scary Night.* London: Walker Books

Maris, R. (1986) *I wish I could fly.* London: Picture Puffins